Contents

Hearing

Our world is full of sound. We hear people talking, birds singing and phones ringing. There are noisy sounds, too. Shouting and slamming doors make loud sounds.

A racing car's engine makes a loud noise.

OUR FIVE SENSES

Popcorn

Comhairle Contae
Átha Cliath Theas
South Dublin County Council

LIBRARY SERVICES ONLINE at www.southdublinlibraries.ie

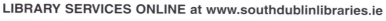

Items should be returned on or before the last date below. Fines, as displayed in the Library, will be charged on overdue items. You may renew your items in person, online at www.southdublinlibraries, or by phone.

Sally Morgan

WAYLAND

Explore the world with **Popcorn** - your complete first non-fiction library.

Look out for more titles in the **Popcorn** range. All books have the same format of simple text and awesome images. Text is carefully matched to the pictures to help readers to identify and understand key vocabulary.
www.waylandbooks.co.uk/popcorn

Published in 2015 by Wayland
Copyright Wayland 2015

Wayland
Hachette Children's Books
338 Euston Road
London NW13BH

Wayland Australia
Level 17/207 Kent Street
Sydney NSW 2000

Editor: Nicola Edwards
Designer: Robert Walster
Picture researcher: Shelley Noronha
Series consultant: Kate Ruttle
Design concept: Paul Cherrill

British Library Cataloguing in Publication Data
Morgan, Sally
  Hearing. - (Popcorn. Five senses)
  1. Hearing - Juvenile literature 2. Sound - Juvenile literature
I. Title
612.8'5
ISBN: 978 0 7502 9463 8

Printed and bound in China

Wayland is a division of Hachette Children's Books, an Hachette UK Company
www.hachette.co.uk

Photographs:
Cover, 18 istockphoto; title page © Joson/zefa/Corbis; 2, 15 James Steidl/istockphoto; 4 Mark Evans/istockphoto; 5 Rich Legg/istock; 6 © Will & Deni McIntyre/Corbis; 7 © Ned Frisk/Corbis; 9, 10, 12, 20, 23 Martyn f. Chillmaid; 11 Ecoscene/Karl Ammann; 13 Ecoscene/Dennis Johnson; 14 Paul Avis/Getty Images; 16 © epa/Corbis; 17 Ecoscene/Alan Towse; 19 Ecoscene/Brian Cushing; 21 © Richard T. Nowitz/Corbis; 22 (tl) Ecoscene/Michael Maconachie; (tr) 22 039081 Ecoscene/Fritz Polking; (bl) Daniel Cardiff/istockphoto; (br) Galina Barskaya/istockphoto

Hearing is one of our five senses.
We hear sounds with our ears.

We use our ears when we listen to somebody talking.

Our five senses
are hearing, sight,
taste, touch
and smell.

Everyday sounds

We use different words to describe sounds. Sounds can be loud or soft. They can bang, pop, ring or rattle.

Can you think of words to describe all the sounds you would hear in this busy street?

We enjoy listening to some sounds, such as musical sounds. Noise is a jumble of loud, harsh sounds which are not pleasant to hear.

People enjoy making and listening to music.

Each musical instrument makes a different sound.

 Our ears

We have two ears. There is one ear on each side of your head. Look at the shape of your ear in a mirror.

The ear's funnel shape makes it good at collecting sounds.

When the ear hears a sound,
a message passes to the brain.
The brain identifies the sound.

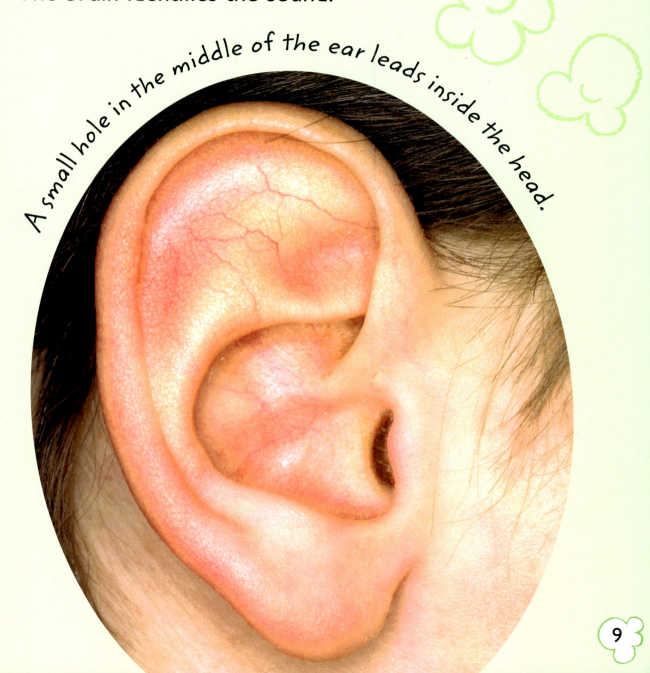

A small hole in the middle of the ear leads inside the head.

 Animal ears

Ears come in different shapes and sizes. Animals with very good hearing usually have large ears.

Rabbits have long, upright ears which can hear quiet sounds.

Elephants can hear very well. They have the largest ears of any animal.

Elephants can flap their ears to help them to keep cool.

Which direction?

If a sound comes from the left, the sound reaches the left ear first. A sound from the right reaches the right ear first.

If you cover one ear, it is more difficult to work out the direction of a sound.

A sound that comes from in front or from behind, reaches both ears at the same time.

Zebras can point their ears forward to hear sounds more clearly.

Loud sounds

Loud sounds are easy to hear. The rumble of a loud explosion or thunder can be heard from far away.

In stormy weather we see lightning and then we hear thunder.

The sirens of police cars and fire engines make loud sounds. When people hear the siren they move out of the way.

The siren of a fire engine sounds louder as it gets nearer and gets quieter as it moves away.

 Danger!

Sounds can be dangerous. If we listen to loud sounds for a long time, we can damage our hearing.

Some musicians wear ear plugs to protect their hearing.

People working in noisy places, such as airports and building sites, have to protect their ears.

This worker is wearing ear guards to protect his ears from the noise of the drill.

Quiet sounds

Some sounds are quiet. Rain falling into puddles, cats padding across the floor and leaves rustling in the wind are quiet sounds.

Whispering is talking very softly, so nobody else can hear.

Large ears trap more sounds. If you cup your hand around your ear, the funnel shape makes sounds louder and easier to hear.

With their large ears, bat-eared foxes can hear insects moving about at night.

Some animals have extra-large ears so they can hear quiet sounds.

Hearing problems

Some people with hearing problems wear a hearing aid. A hearing aid picks up sounds and makes them louder.

A hearing aid helps this girl to hear what her teacher is saying.

Some people cannot hear at all.
They use their fingers to talk to
other people in sign language.

These children are learning how to use sign language.

21

Match the sounds

Can you match the sound to the animal?

Woof!

Roar! *Quack!*

Hiss!

Play a game with your family or friends. Make the sound of one of these animals and see if they can guess the name of the animal.

Improve your hearing

You will need:
- a square piece of stiff paper
- scissors
- sticky tape.

Find out how you can make sounds louder and easier to hear. Roll a piece of paper into the shape of a cone, or funnel, and fasten it with sticky tape.

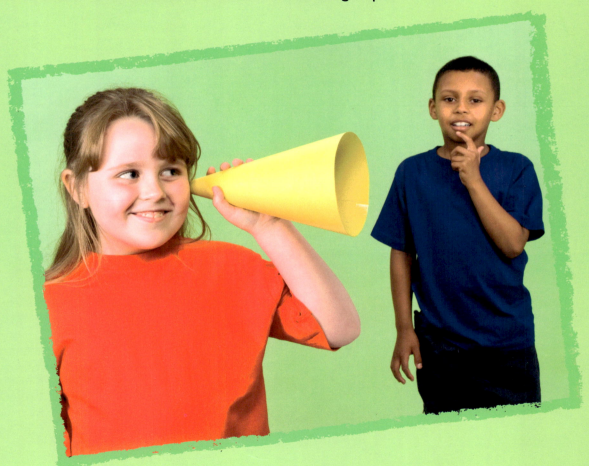

Ask a friend to stand on the other side of the room and whisper something. Can you hear them?

Glossary

brain the control centre of the body, found inside the head

ear guards coverings for the ears that protect them from loud noise

ear plugs small pieces of plastic worn inside the ears to protect them from loud sounds

funnel a cone-shaped device that is wide at one end and narrow at the other

hearing aid a device that people can wear in their ears to help them hear better

senses functions of the body through which we gather information about our surroundings

sign language a way of talking to someone by using hand shapes

Index